ALL ABOUT PDA

An Insight Into
Pathological Demand Avoidance

KATHY HOOPMANN

Jessica Kingsley Publishers
London and Philadelphia

A NOTE FROM THE AUTHOR

When I first considered writing a book on Pathological Demand Avoidance (PDA), my first thought was, "Is there a need for it?" To find out, I approached the experts – PDAers themselves – and I was resoundingly told, "Yes! We need others to know about us, to understand us and realise we are not trying to be difficult. Please write this book." Likewise, when I approached those who lived and worked with PDAers, they said, "We want people to know that PDAers are amazing people who help us re-evaluate our philosophies and approaches to life and may well be the catalyst for systemic change to education and welfare that benefits all. Please write this book!"

So, I wrote this book.

PDA, first identified by psychologist Elizabeth Newson in the 1980s, is a diagnosis in progress. PDAers exhibit an extreme resistance to, or avoidance of, the everyday demands of life – even activities they may enjoy – based on a need to feel in control when anxious or stressed. It is not recognised on the DSM-5, and various specialists have different views about what it is and how it plays out in life. There is a consensus that it is a profile of autism, and it certainly shows up mostly under the autistic umbrella.

However, some researchers suggest that there are PDA links to ADHD and other diagnoses as well, and some believe it is a stand-alone condition. Likewise, the language around PDA is constantly adapting and changing. Even the term *Pathological Demand Avoidance* has its nay-sayers, with alternative preferences including *Pervasive Drive for Autonomy*, *Persistent Drive for Autonomy*, *Pervasive Demand Avoidance* or *Extreme Demand Avoidance*, among others. Currently, the term *Pathological Demand Avoidance* is used for the sake of continuity and clarity, although that may change in the future. So, taking into consideration all those views, *All About PDA* is written with the best intentions to capture the essence of PDA as it is understood at the time of writing.

I could not have written this book alone. I am very grateful to those in the PDA community who have given enormous amounts of their time, wisdom and story-sharing to help me create a book that will hopefully help demystify a complex and rare diagnosis. Any mistakes that remain are mine alone.

A massive thanks goes to Heidi Brandis (Founder of PDA Perth WA Parents Community and Support Group) and Sally Canadine (PDA Talk), who patiently spent hours and hours helping me fine-tune the language and correct the grammar and who were not afraid to tell me when I got things wrong. I simply could not have written this book without them.

Kylie Reeve, thank you for finding the gentlest and kindest way to inform me that my first draft needed serious work. This book is so much better for your velvet-fisted honesty. I am also grateful to so many people for their encouragement and enthusiasm for this project; for sitting with me over coffee and sharing their lives; for allowing me to interview them; and for patiently editing draft after draft. My deep gratitude goes to the following people, in no particular order: Tony Attwood, Michelle Garnett, Theresa Kidd, Zoe Martin, Tracey Churchill, Chris Hausler and AJ, Helen Evans, Summer Farrelly, Rosa Minns, Laura Kerbey, Penny Hood, Rebecca Houkamau and my ever-patient husband, Errol Hoopmann.

What is Pathological Demand Avoidance?

Glad you asked.

At first glance, it's easy to understand.

Those with PDA, or PDAers, simply experience and interpret the world differently from those around them.

However, the way their brains work is clever and complex and that is much trickier to explain.

3

For a start, PDA is a profile of autism, but PDAers may not react and behave like many other autistic people.

Sure, they may share some autistic traits, like being sensitive to noises, smells, touch and taste, and they might prefer to avoid those who don't even try to understand them.

Yet PDA is so much more than trying to avoid people, places and things.

It's all about how pressured and threatened PDAers feel when they are not in control of their own lives.

So, to keep that control, they resist and avoid demands put on them.

Do you know how many demands are made every single day?

Laws
and lists
and rules
and signs
and plans
and charts
and menus
and recipes
and agendas
and timetables
and instructions
can all be demands
that feel threatening.

What is not so obvious are hidden demands.

When people say they know what PDAers would like or want, it's as if they are telling them what they should think and feel.

Even being thanked or praised might make them feel pressured to do the same thing again, giving the other person control over them.

PDAers love having friends, so they often try hard to fit in, which can also be very demanding.

I can't keep this up for long.

Some find there is less pressure to have just one friend at a time who plays only with them, their way.

Being tempted with a reward can increase anxiety. A demand, plus the added pressure of working for a treat, is all too much!

PDAers are quite sensitive and may think people are really angry when they are only a little cross or frustrated.

If someone yells or barks a demand, a PDAer's anxiety can skyrocket.

For some PDAers, even feeling hungry or thirsty, needing to sleep, being hot or cold, or wanting to go to the toilet are all demands that their own bodies make on them.

For a while, when a PDAer's anxiety is low and they feel safe, they may be able to say "OK" to some requests and hidden demands.

At other times, the same things are overwhelming, and they have to say **"No!"**

It's not that PDAers **aren't capable** of following an instruction.
At that moment, they're **not able** to, even though they might
have done it before and they know exactly **how** to do it.

In fact, if they're told to do something that they were already going to do, then it may stop them doing it!

And it's not about trying to get out of work or chores, as sometimes they can't even go to places they enjoy or do things they love to do.

But you loved it last time.

It's just that, for some PDAers, it's like a demand freezes their computer screen and they need to feel safe, calm and in control before it will work again.

22

To reduce their anxiety, PDAers might first ignore requests, or promise to do them later, hoping they will go away.

Some PDAers are very good at switching topics,

or making people laugh so a request might be forgotten.

I can't go out because I might get sucked up by aliens and be taken to the mooooon!

They may give funny or clever reasons for not following a request,

or create fantasy worlds where a demand is no longer possible.

As PDAers find more and more reasons to avoid requests to reduce their anxiety, it helps if those around them remain calm.

Yet, often, the more PDAers resist, the more others insist.

And the more others insist, the more PDAers resist.

Some PDAers might run away.
Anything, **anything** to stop the demands.

Others may try to stop all the frightened, running-away feelings by curling up in a ball and hiding.

If the demands or rules or requests don't
stop, then anxiety builds up and up.

For PDAers, it's as if there is a terrible attack on
their safety and they must fight for survival.

Without warning, they may meltdown, and yell or hit or break things.

They have no control over when this happens or what triggers it.

When the meltdown is over, they might feel sad and exhausted. Sometimes they have no memory of what was said and done.

Going to a safe place with a trusted person nearby, where they can do something that they choose, may help them to calm down.

If they are expected to say sorry – as if the things done during the meltdown were on purpose – they may not be able to, so no one knows how much they regret upsetting those they love.

There are times when some people don't understand PDAers and PDAers don't understand others. It can be hard for everyone.

But it doesn't have to be that way. There are many things that help PDAers feel in control.

If demands are lifted, then pressures and threats are eased.

Although, if someone tries to trick them to do something by making a demand not sound like a demand, then it won't work. They're too clever for that!

It can be helpful to give them a choice when they are calm.

However, if their anxiety is high, then the same choice may become a demand.

On the other hand, if they are given too many choices, they may freeze, and prefer that someone else decides.

If it's possible for them to say "No," then it's easier to say "Yes".

Let's make funny faces before we get dressed.

Some PDAers love doing things on a whim. If it's fun, then even better.

Today

- ☐ Bed
- ☐ Bins
- ☐ Dinner

Tasks may be less threatening if written on a board or in texts, or if someone points rather than speaks.

And if a request comes from a puppet or toy, then it may be more fun to go along with it.

I wonder if anyone can help my poor nose by taking out the smelly rubbish?

The law says we must wear a seat belt.

If the people making the demand have no choice themselves, then PDAers may find it less stressful to follow, as they are both in the same situation.

PDAers are natural leaders, so it helps if those around them show genuine interest in the things they love, but don't take charge.

When PDAers trust someone and feel safe with them, they are more likely to follow their requests.

They don't follow someone just because that person might be older or an authority over them.

Even so, if they're passionate about learning something, then allowing a coach or a teacher to lead them becomes easier, because it is their choice to be there.

PDAers manage best if they can have their say.

The more they are in control of their own lives, and the more that people understand and support them, the calmer they feel.

And then their many skills and strengths can shine.

PDAers can be strong-willed, brave and curious,

with extraordinary imaginations and creative talents.

They're often quirky, witty and cheeky,

and can be delightful and entertaining company.

Being very independent, they prefer to discover things for themselves,

Maybe I'll bring a jacket next time.

and some learn better from real life,
rather than from a book or screen.

Many are brilliant at absorbing facts on
their own and at their own pace,

and may astonish those around them with their knowledge.

How do you know that!?

When they find something that captures their interest, they can become hyper-focused,

and through determination and persistence, they can excel, often in unique ways.

They may be sensitive and affectionate and have an incredible sense of justice.

If life is unfair, for them or for others, they will stand up for what is right.

63

As they grow older, PDAers may teach the things they are passionate about or sell what they create.

They might start their own businesses or online activities, or volunteer to help others. Some may have jobs with bosses, and some may not.

Whatever they choose to do or however they spend their time, with understanding and acceptance from those around them, life can get better and better!

Animal names and photograph credits

Page 33
Lion Cub © nwdph

Page 44
Tricolor Australian Shepherd © Mark Herreid

Page 55
Border Collie © dezy

Page 34
Panda © Hung Chung Chih

Page 45
Puppet © TK6photo

Page 56
Monkey © north-tail

Page 35
Meerkats © Anton Watman

Page 46
Pug © Sylvie Pabion Martin

Page 57
Ground Squirrel © Barbora Polivkova

Page 36
Chimpanzee © Tabish Hassan Khan

Page 47
Goats © Rita_Kochmarjova

Page 58
Owl © New Africa

Page 37
Rabbits © Rita_Kochmarjova

Page 48
Shetland Pony with Kitten © Rita_Kochmarjova

Page 59
Ground Squirrel © Jan Stria

Page 38
Four-toed Hedgehog © Kuttelvaserova Stuchelova

Page 49
Rainbow Lorikeets © QuickStartProjects

Page 60
Sheep © FOTOGRIN

Page 39
Ambilobe Panther Chameleon, Veiled Chameleon © Cathy Keifer

Page 50
Orangutans © Nagel Photography

Page 61
Giraffe © Krakenimages.com

Page 40
Ring-tailed Lemur © Wang LiQiang

Page 51
Koalas © Andras Deak

Page 62
Koalas © UX Pictures

Page 41
Arctic Hare © SofieLion

Page 52
Raccoon © Vasyan_23

Page 63
Meerkats © Nika_Z

Page 42
Giraffes © Vladimir Turkenich

Page 53
Horse © urfin

Page 64
Lion Cub © Volodymyr Burdiak

Page 43
Giraffe © WildStrawberry

Page 54
Ram © Jan Krava

Page 65
Quokka © Hideaki Edo Photography

First published in Great Britain in 2025 by Jessica Kingsley Publishers
An imprint of John Murray Press

1

Copyright © Kathy Hoopmann 2025

The right of Kathy Hoopmann to be identified as the Author
of the Work has been asserted by her in accordance with
the Copyright, Designs and Patents Act 1988.

All photographs courtesy of Shutterstock.co.uk

The fonts, layout and overall design of this book have been prepared
according to dyslexia-friendly principles. At JKP we aim to make our
books' content accessible to as many readers as possible.

A CIP catalogue record for this title is available from the
British Library and the Library of Congress

ISBN 978 1 83997 756 5
eISBN 978 1 83997 757 2

Printed and bound in China by Leo Paper Products

Jessica Kingsley Publishers' policy is to use papers that are
natural, renewable and recyclable products and made from wood
grown in sustainable forests. The logging and manufacturing
processes are expected to conform to the environmental
regulations of the country of origin.

Jessica Kingsley Publishers
Carmelite House
50 Victoria Embankment
London EC4Y 0DZ

www.jkp.com

John Murray Press
Part of Hodder & Stoughton Ltd
An Hachette Company

by the same author

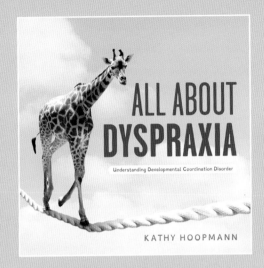

All About Dyspraxia
ISBN 978 1 78775 835 3 | eISBN 978 1 78775 836 0

All Dogs Have ADHD
ISBN 978 1 78775 660 1 | eISBN 978 1 78775 661 8

All Cats Are on the Autism Spectrum
ISBN 978 1 78775 471 3 | eISBN 978 1 78775 472 0

All Birds Have Anxiety
ISBN 978 1 78592 182 7 | eISBN 978 1 78450 454 0